Rumors of Wisdom

Rumors of Wisdom

Jerome Gagnon

Concrete Wolf
Louis Award Series

Copyright © 2019 Jerome Gagnon

All rights reserved. No part of this publication may be reproduced, distributed, or transmitted in any form or by any means whatsoever without written permission from the publisher, except in the case of brief excerpts for critical reviews and articles. All inquiries should be addressed to Concrete Wolf Press.

Concrete Wolf Louis Award Series

Poetry
ISBN 978-0-9964754-7-1

Design: Tonya Namura using Minion Pro

Cover photo: excerpt from *Moonrise in perigee* by Krückstock, wiki commons

Author photo by Mary Sanchez

Concrete Wolf
PO Box 445
Tillamook, OR 97141

http://ConcreteWolf.com

ConcreteWolfPress@gmail.com

For my mother and father

Table of Contents

I Spell of the Ordinary
Looking Out at the Stream	5
Joice Street Steps	6
Absence of Poppies	7
Shed	8
Spotting Turkeys	9
Still Life with Lemons	10
Barometer	11
This Cup	12
Gifts	13
Praise for Gray	14
Crow Makes a Scene	15
First Frost	16
Laundry Day	17
Pulling Weeds	18
Yellow House	19
Noted in Passing	20
After Vowing	21
What Would You Call It?	22
Cherries, After	23

II Uncertain Fire
In This Fire	27
December Mushrooms	28
Uncertain Fire	29
Survivors	30
Geocarpy of Longing	31
A Walk in the Park	32
Winter Moon	33
Sweetfire in Peach Season	34
Why Poetry?	35
Ekphrasis	36
Pyrography	37
Another Word About It	38

Cranking the Wheel	39
Pieces, Some Blue	40
Elegy for a Stray Cat	41
The Soul Longs for Home	42
Stripping Wallpaper	43

III Rumors of Wisdom

Praising Chair	47
The Good Knot	48
Crossings	49
Evening Rain	50
Bonsai	51
Praising Names	52
Bright Morning	53
Ladder	54
Why We Sing in the Shower	55
In the Antique Store Yesterday,	56
Butter and Egg Days	57
In the Lobby of Hotel Paradise	58
Up a Creek	59
Beginnings	60
Persimmon Tree	61
Some Ways into Joy	62
Milkweed Wishes	63
Blackbirds in December	64
Self	65
Dry Spell	66
Something of What Was	67
White Poppies	68
Acknowledgements	69
About the Author	71

Rumors of Wisdom

I

Spell of the Ordinary

Looking Out at the Stream

which is really not a stream
but a dried river bed that we installed last summer,
carrying bucketsful of mixed gravel
which are really bits and pieces of the last ice age
that came rushing out of nowhere
in a great, white wave of change,
I noticed that some dried bamboo leaves on the ground
resembled little canoes piled up on the imaginary shore,
and then forgot all about it until now,
trying to make something more of it,
of the mind's preoccupation with metaphor,
of the need to know, to explain the inexplicable,
the world as it is —

grateful for failing that, again.

Joice Street Steps

When you climb this stair, at first it doesn't seem
a way to anywhere, although the yellow and blue
wildflowers that poke out of the mossy risers
this time of year offer their usual message of — what —
renewal? Arrival?

If you know it's there, the little altar half-way up,
you may anticipate what offerings have been given,
although there's always the fear that it may be gone
or ruined.

But it's intact and so are you —
a threadbare shelf with a few plastic flowers on it,
and an image notable more for its feeling
than its artistry, for what remains unseen.

Plainly, this is an homage to the queen of mothers
(her face could be a wing or anything living,
her face could be a prayer),
and without willing it you may find yourself

offering some silent words of praise, or thanks,
or remembrance before passing through
the airy chamber where — whose? — footsteps
have paused from the climb and what
has been stilled continues, only lighter.

Absence of Poppies

How and why a house goes abandoned
is everybody's business:

most say there was a problem with a will
or a falling-out, or both.
It's just wrong, they say, to let a house go like this.

I don't know, but every day I pass by it in June,
I gape at the tangled overgrowth, wrapping the porch
with dozens of white flowers — the matilija —

their glowing petals held together by an equal number
of button-sized suns, and I want to unbutton them all,
enter the secret of their luminescence,

not thinking how paradise blooms in absence,
how the black bee revels in the unkempt blossoms —
their nectar as sweet as anything kempt —

how mice have their field day here,
and gossips theirs, and the spotted owl its mice,
when all around and in the house

darkness resumes, and the swaying poppies
have folded in on themselves,
still holding onto their burning secret.

Shed

So this is where the broom has gone to rest,
leaning against the shed,
its one straw wing bent to the ground,

where the rusted pick-axe, its handle lost to time,
keeps the latch-less door closed to possums and others
but mostly to wind.

No one really wants to go in there, I don't think,
lifting aside the axe which reminds me of an anchor,
the shed a battered hull that's somehow washed ashore.

Not expecting to find among the cobwebs
and shards of insect wings, the bottles of fertilizers
and poisons — on a dusty shelf in the corner —

the rainbow glow of an abalone shell,
the familiar face staring back like a forgotten lover,
patient, and slow to happiness.

Spotting Turkeys

Last night's rain has flattened the grass
where a rafter of wild turkeys inches along,
        bowing as they go —
content to do just what turkeys do,
to be just who or what they are,
egg-born, bony, and humble as dirt.

They linger on the hillside with a deep thrum,
feathered instruments tuning up in bass,
assessing all in their ken:
                glossy seedlings,
bent stalks of milkweed,
copper-green lichen on a rock.

            Pecking and scrutinizing
at the edges of things
as if they had all the time in the world.

                Then, crackling,
lively as fire,
      they spread across the hillside,
           darkening it with mystery.

When they leave with a low ascent
and muffled clapping, the landscape listens —
        rapt, in their spell.

Still Life with Lemons

Lemons in a glass bowl, centered on a white tablecloth,
could mean anything — lemonade, a lemon cake?

Someone, I think I know who, has offered them,
plucked or cut them neatly from their stems,
except for the one resting on top with its nubby cord
and double leaf like elongated butterfly wings —

like nothing you may have ever seen, except in books,
The Big Book of Butterflies, although that one had zebra stripes
and may actually have been a moth.

What could they mean, these uncomplicated lemons,
so yellow, so waxy-perfect,
as if posing for a still-life, a gouache?

They're the flowers' answer to the same old question,
but that's side-stepping the issue, isn't it?

Are they meant for pleasure, then? For beauty?
For their fiery seed, to turn the wheel once more?
Or are they meant for bitterness alone?

Cutting into soft rind, I inhale summer's fragrance —
sweetest clover, verbena,
                dusty folds of marigolds —

and something almost forgotten, not yet forgotten,
in the hollow of my chest
                            exults
as if drenched in a warm rain.

Barometer

It's true I no longer need you,
what with the speed of today's search engines,
air pressure and temperature at my fingertips,
but I'd still rather run them along the curve
of your mahogany casing
as you define the world in percentages and arrows,
wondering if you aren't a distant cousin of the violin,
unmusical but good with numbers,
although, I have to say, I've also wondered at times
if you weren't hiding something behind the glass,
some vital information that might be measured
by a hidden gauge that could have warned me
who would be lost early on and who would be left behind,
and another that pointed to the level of remorse
that might be expected, based on any number of variables —

portents of an uncertain life, lived just the same,
surer in some small degree with you hanging there
on a wall by the door.

This Cup

All through lunch I've gazed at this cup,
taking baby sips of steaming, green tea,
and now, I think,
I may be in love with it.

Glazed patches of mottled brown
and turquoise like chameleons' skin —
evidence of the enduring mutable,
set by the kiln.

Handy indentations for hands to grip,
outside and inside much the same.
On the bottom, an indecipherable
maker's name.

Crazy to love a cup, I know,
and not a wife,
but all through lunch I've been gazing
and holding on for dear life.

Gifts

They've come so far to be here
this one time,
slice of a moment we notice briefly
before it passes into something else,
expecting the usual curves they bring us,
the subtle flesh scent
as we come to them, not in awe, exactly,
but more in gratitude
for how they've suddenly ripened,
for their promised sweetness,
and not especially for the shifting umbras
that help to define them
but which are still notable —

these two late and freckled pears,
gleaming on a windowsill.

Praise for Gray

There's much to be said for an overcast day.
Photographs come out better.
It gives us something to measure our sunny days by
but who's counting?
Not the dove who wears it as an overcoat, beating
her woolen sleeves as she flies from the nest,
or the ivy leaf that bends with each drop
from the tree, above.

A good day for chopping wood,
for walking up or down a hill,
for reading a novel about unrequited love,
for polishing shoes to a dull shine,
for reorganizing the mind's closets,
for baking almost anything,
especially apples.

All of which I forgo to write a poem
whose only purpose is praise for a familiar hand
that stills the air between words
and blurs the edges of the known.

Crow Makes a Scene

in the puddle where the old elm stood,
splashing and crowing for anyone who'll listen
to her chorus of wings on water, water on wings,
and the guttural praise of something wild,
unfettered.

I watch as she lifts, flying low to the ground,
and circles back, still crowing about the occurrence
of water that appears out of nothing —
cool, black mirror that must be broken, again,
before it takes her into its dark splendor.

First Frost

                                This morning
I feel just as if I'd stepped out of a paper sack,
staring at this glittering world with disbelief —

gessoed rooftops, sidewalks and lawns,
slickened branches, noble pines
                         and drooping bamboo,
all of them dancing with fractured light,
diamond light —

not knowing where frost leaves off and fire begins
or even what to call this
stinging bliss.

There must be hundreds of kinds of happiness
and most of us know so few of them.
Shouldn't we at least know their names?

Or if not that, act as if we do,
as if we've known them all our lives,
welcoming them with open arms when they come to us
unannounced, possibly icy and aflame,
and then watch them change, as they will,
into something else:

wisps of steam, twisting
like ghost-dancers on the rooftops;
silvered branches of the coral maple, seguing to red;
the silent witness, melting in dusty rivulets
from the windowsill.

Laundry Day

Standing next to the churning washer,
turning the sleeve of a shirt right-side out,
I felt myself turning, also —
the two of us of the same piece of cloth.

How long I stood there,
and how it was that this plaid, cotton shirt and I
came to be the soiled fabric of the world,
who can say?

Pulling Weeds

Beneath a layer of gravel and black plastic,
seeds of a meadow have poked their way
through to the light — violet stalks
topped with flaming yellow
and imperfect circles of the future
in the form of so much fluff.

                         Kneeling, I grasp each one
at the root, shaking damp earth loose,
remembering inky blackbirds
that once roosted in these ancestral weeds —
their red markings revealed
as tiny sparks in flight —

considering just who the intruder is,
as a mist touches everything.

Yellow House

Yesterday, I saw for the first time
the little yellow house
with the jacaranda in front of it,
purple petals spread about
on the sidewalk and in the branches,
although I can't say which I saw first,
house or tree.

We joined in song right away.
First the two of them,
the yellow house meting out rhythm
to the pulsing lyric of the jacaranda,
and then the impromptu backup sighing,

Oh baby, Oh baby,
all day and all night long.

Noted in Passing

The message is everywhere —
last week as I passed by a neighbor's yard, scanning roses,
the silence broken by a siren growing louder and louder,
and then, finally, an ambulance turning the corner
and pulling up just two houses away.

Then yesterday, running to catch a bus,
avoiding a crushed blackbird —
the work of a red-tailed hawk or an owl, probably —
as I stepped across a blanket of white flowers,
fallen from a tree I never knew blossomed.

In the funnel of a flower, sky flecked with ash;
the sufficiency of each in the other.

After Vowing

not to write anything more about hummingbirds,
I slip up, asking whether
it's mainly about the blur of tiny wings
or its uncanny performance,
the way it stays suspended
in mid-air —
a quivering question mark
with a
fluted beak —

or if it's more about the sheen of green satin
that spreads from its breast
to the dome of its head,
or its quick oblations to the trumpet flower
as it darts in and out
to extract the nectar there,

or if there's something other
than wonder that draws us in its sphere,
leaving us suspended, too,
until it disappears?

A fury of light, call it,
flickering between wing beats,
that shines clear through from the bone,
granting,
not answers, necessarily,
but this
swift and feathered
transparency.

What Would You Call It?

Other than the usual call that beauty or desire
are what keep us spellbound by the fire
and gazing into the beloved's eyes, there's the bushtit,
riding the back of the mare, pecking lice;

the grassfire last summer that left stumps of scrub
and laurel, charred bed where the matilija poppy
lifts its white, saucer-sized flowers —
beautiful, yes, but not the point.

Would you call it symbiosis that joins bird and horse,
and feeds the poppy, or would you call it providence?
No doubt you have your ideas just as I do,
and we could discuss the nuances ad infinitum.

                                                But listen,
a friend who notices these things tells me
that the bud of the matilija opens to the sun
with a pop like breaking bread,
a process that takes seventeen seconds, she says,

and also occurs in moonlight.

Cherries, After

The bucket from the shed where something scurried
is badly rusted, and the ladder that leaned against the door
is twisted and light, made from cherry wood.

You can smell it in the flickering between the trees
as you reach for cherries, ripe and happy in the leaves,
the faintly sour taste of cherry on your tongue and breath
but mostly sweet, mostly sweet.

And each bucket you fill you pour in your sack,
going back for more, even though your arms are burning
and you're thinking about sleeping in the shade of the trees
for a while, up against the cool, flat part of a trunk,

and you do, lulled by the hum of bees
and the clicking of blackbirds, not thinking anything
like cherries are the mirror of summer,
although you could say that if you wanted to —

something about the glint off most every one
like stars reflected on a glassy bay off Massachusetts
or Maine or New Hampshire, and, of course, you do —

still dreaming these many years later
about the promise of cherries,
darkly gleaming in a russet sack.

II

Uncertain Fire

In This Fire

is a roving eye that scans the world
in search of dry grasses,
the still bodies of leaves
and bundled longings,

returning again and again
to its familiar haunt beneath the mantel
with the silent clock
and jasper vase, other eyes

that welcome it through the night,
baring evidence of grief
and faith in something bright
that dances while it burns.

December Mushrooms

Shouldn't they be called *sunset moon,*
or maybe *harvest moon* for their orangey caps?

I only know they're new here
in what was once the town square, clustered
in the fractured light beneath an elm,
carried in with truckloads of shredded bark
and nurtured by a deluge of rain.

I'm careful to step around them,
yet can't help but touch and gently lift a bendable cap,
exposing the spaghetti-like stem —
pretty package.
Who knows, though, what secret it holds?

Crow and squirrel leave it alone,
even insects resist its lunar spell.

Uncertain Fire

I don't think fire knows where it's headed
when it jumps from limb to limb, house to house.
Yet, like a dog following a scent,
sometimes it seems to consider a spark of itself
on an adjacent roof or branch before it leaps
and is off and running.
Towards what — home or prey?

It couldn't be love, how could it?
Although, afterwards, in the televised stink
of devastation, someone may say the familiar words,
how grateful they were that they lived through it,
got out with just the clothes on their back
or a dazed bird in a cage,
the cat missing.

Or that they found something, weeks later,
in the debris where the old life stood —
a melted buckle or piece of a photo, say,
that reminded them of fire's power,
how everything alters or vanishes in its path.

And I think, even the wish, *if only*,
even the question, *why?*

Survivors

1.
If you ask how I did it, I'd say:
"It was luck," or "grace," or "timing."
The truth is, I don't know.
Time isn't real, someone once said, but it is
if you're waiting in line for a new heart
or the new cocktail.

2.
After everyone I didn't know I loved
and most of those I did were gone,
someone stepped out of a pool of shadows,
not exactly a stranger,
not exactly him, or her, or everyone.
Brother, I want to say. Sister.

3.
It's a sad business that pairs memory with loss —
honeybee boxing with a cobweb.
When I remember the gone world now,
I don't think so much about this or that
but of the light that shines in everything
like a flame seen through crazed glass.

Geocarpy of Longing

1.
The way we come to wisdom lies hidden
like dehiscent fruit that grows in the ground:
each of us a kindred seed that ripens in the dark.

2.
In the womb of the calyx, our need is for fire and light.
Stilled to all else, we wait in the waiting.

3.
This quiet becoming is a coming forth, but also a joining
of earth and air, and the dim memory of a field
where hands bear flowers in the shapes of stars —
fulfillment of an old promise.

4.
The taste of our fruits is the taste of the world
giving itself to itself,
and to the scatterings of birds who praise them.

5.
This is the season of doubt for all we've borne,
for our winter of despair and the icy spring
that felt like our undoing, that was our undoing.
If not that, what, then?
We're here, aren't we, and crowning.

A Walk in the Park

> *What's a simple crime of property*
> *when life, breath, and all*
> *is at stake?*
> — Linda Hogan

Not much bad happened here,
and much that sings.

Well, there were two drunken friends,
the papers said, one assaulted the other
in a nearby field one night.

Then this in broad daylight:

SUSPECT IN CAR THEFT
SHOT DEAD BY POLICE

Somebody scrawled *Peace* in blue chalk
on the sidewalk and drew a heart around it,
and flowers in bottles and cans appeared
for days afterward,

under the sheening trees where he fell.

Winter Moon

Haven't we lost our silvering, old friend,
tarnished like the gravy spoon
in the back of the drawer?

And where have they gone,
those bright whisperings?

Among pewtered eucalyptus and scarred bark,
in salt cliffs and dune whirls,
rushing and still waters,

on sequined koi,
wings of snow geese and cyclamen,

into the night, drifting with star-powder
and sea-sparkle,
discarded selves and slivered ice.

Don't you feel it —
the chill flame licking at your heart?

Watch as we spill, one into another,
before morning comes with its shiver
and glisten.

Sweetfire in Peach Season

Somewhere it's peach season.
Light falls across the orchard, inventing shadows,
and the dog laps at the fountain.

Let it come to you, then, the leafy dream of morning
with its many openings and paths,
star-glazed pebbles,
clusters of peaches and flowers,
a few dawdling flowers,
their heady scent everywhere,

noting how perfectly it fits in your hand,
                                    summer's prize,
as if it was a part of you, peach skin
warm with the breath of the sun,
such delicious warmth, too,
sweetfire, call it,

and all the while the grazing of the bow,
drawing out the piercing decrescendo —

three notes in a minor key
        from a lonely praiser
                somewhere in the branches —

has you peach-struck, and *oh*,
burning, burning.

Why Poetry?

Because it offers a way to address the snail
without being accused of lunacy.

Because it honors the wild and the gone.

Because it reminds me of what I've known
all along but often forget: that language is music
as much as the bee's thrum,
the dog's bark,
the cricket's song —

each of us playing and played upon
in the audible dark.

Ekphrasis
    inspired by Georg Flegel's *Dessert Still Life*

1.
In a still life with grapes and other points of interest,
the eye goes to a glass chalice on a tabletop,
notices how those grapes glisten, though not more so
than the chalice, sparked by ceremonies of light;
how just a few arcs of white, scrapings really,
stoke our curiosity.
You almost have to dip a finger in to find out
if it's empty or not, so fragile is the distinction
between glass and wine.
Ask yourself if we aren't like that, holding emptiness
in an invisible embrace, downing it
in a thirst for light.

2.
But this is only part of the picture.
That stilted parrot, for instance, why is it robed
in the varnished dark?
The white dot on the eye of the mouse
offers a glimmer of an answer.

3.
Is it greed that gives the gray mouse its appetite
for sticky fruits and nutmeats?
Or is it desire, the dark in the light that enthralls us
and gives us weight?

Pyrography

Trailing vines on canted pedestals,
blossoming picture frames, trays
and boxes for sweet things to be kept
on mantels, mantels themselves.

Almost anything wooden you might want
to lay your hands and eyes on,
all of them scorched and varnished
until they shine like clear night with a
sprinkling of stars.

Much as love burns its name on the gnarled
root of the heart.
First, everything warms up, then,
the gentle tracery that feels like plumule
on the underside of the skin.

Before the nuzzling that starts you singing,
before the sizzling that has you wondering
who you've become, and how
will you keep this difficult art burning,
from blowing sky-high — hope
and feathers everywhere.

Another Word About It

The show is dazzling this year, as usual:
downy white and fiery pink petals
tossed in the wind, their honeyed scent everywhere;
translucent leaf curls of the elm;
catkins falling like benevolent messages
from heaven.

The usual suspects are here
on every antenna and branch — each of them
as if vying for a spot on *Nature's Got Talent*,
their multitudinous songs blending
into one enormous heart swell
capable of melting common indifference.

Even so.

My sight is drawn from the fulsome plum
to the still-bare branches around it,
this morning's rain hanging on
like a thousand eyes,
unfooled,
calmly taking it all in.

Cranking the Wheel
   — for my father

as I pulled in the garden hose,
I couldn't help but wonder who or what it is
that pulls us into this blooming world
and then sends us hurling into nothingness.

Or is it we ourselves who turn the wheel,
as I've done this afternoon
after flooding the rhododendron bed
with expectations of scarlet,

just beneath the window of the room
where he sleeps, all but blind now
to beauty and it's entailments.

Pieces, Some Blue

If each piece is a part of something greater than,
like a winter puzzle spread across a table,
then let me gather each of them in,

not only parts of made things
but those that lift out of the land —
wild artichokes rising from cracks in a vacant parking lot,
spiked pods fallen from the branch,
plums that can be shaken off into a long scarf,

what evidence can be found of those borne on the wind —
feathers of hawks and jays, bones of smaller birds,
a frozen nest littered with blue specks.

And let me also take up things given by the roiling
    of waves —
twin halves of shells, full of shining emptiness,
the sand dollar with its cryptic star,
deflated forms of jellyfish aligned with hems of foam,

shadows of creatures that slither and meld in the grass,
all those that awaken, hungry
in the dead of night,

and what shouldn't be forgotten —
what can be gleaned from the wisdom of elders,
tellers of fortunes and stories,
what can be learned from the fires of love.

Elegy for a Stray Cat

I thought once that God couldn't see death,
only knew that falling was a passage into new life.
But now I think that the world suffers when we suffer,
sings when we sing.
That everything that moves with graceful abandon
is the world dancing with itself — the garter snake
curling through grass, bats swooping at sunset,
the old mare on the hill, tossing back her mane.
Which doesn't stave off the shock of it,
your wide-eyed stare,
but opens into this familiar wilderness
where nothing goes unnoticed, nothing is amiss,
and even the stray, the unwanted,
are partnered in mystery.

The Soul Longs for Home

1.
There may come a time, if it hasn't already,
when your heart cracks open,
and no god, no prayer can enter there.
You walk around with this exposed wound at your center.
When you see your face reflected in the window
of a Chinese market — the stoop of your neck,
the way your mouth is painted on like a thin gash —
something deep inside you wants to cry out
about the ache of lost love,
of skinny ducks hanging from hooks on a wire.
Details will vary.

2.
If I say that loss is a pilgrimage
and we don't travel this road alone,
would that be so unthinkable?

3.
One day, you notice the street sweeper
making neat piles of leaves on the sidewalk
is smiling to himself.
Crusty loaves of bread jump out from their wrappers.
The resonance of bees amazes you.
The ground beneath your feet rises up,
and the sky above your head
sends down its airy messages of welcome
to everything — just everything —
but you, in particular.
You go on,
not because.

Stripping Wallpaper

off the front hall where it stuck for decades,
I found it hard not to think of the wet paper
with its acrid smell as history.

That, woven into the fabric were our voices
and those of friends we welcomed in and then waved off
with dulcet goodbyes and exhortations —

and as I scraped the gluey remnants of our lives
from the wall, I thought I heard someone's laughter.
I don't know whose it was.

III

Rumors of Wisdom

Praising Chair

These days, a well-made chair is enough
to give me pause, not for its beauty exactly —
this one's all battered pine legs and peeling green paint,
but *sturdy* —

not for its beauty, per se, but for its intent,
the way it all but asks me to carry it out
into the narrow yard
where there's just enough sunlight this afternoon
to ignite brick walls,
turn camellia leaves to jade,

and I do,
finding comfort in chair, the feel of body to body,
flesh to flesh,
each of us taking on something of the other,
feet planted firmly on the ground —
not listening for the dim voices of birds in the next yard
or anything else for that matter —

leafing

The Good Knot

There is in each of us a hard knot
that must be loosened, fingered
and learned by heart,
so that we can untie it in the dark
of our days and go free.

When we find it, the hands begin
their quiet work of acceptance,
eyes follow every move,
while a voice inside says, No,
this is not it, or *Yes, this is,*

and sings.

Crossings

All day we waited for the ferry that never came,
the seas were too choppy, they said.
When it came the next day, dawn saw us
for what we were, not pilgrims or tourists
with the usual trappings: we were there
for the one-way ticket out.

Like everyone else, we could only guess
that we would arrive safely at our destination
but where that was, exactly, I couldn't say.
Not knowing, either, that the boat would glide
so effortlessly,
like an enormous crate above the waves

that blushed pink under a starry sky,
or how quickly we would forget our names,
why we had come here at all,
if not for this boundless unknowing — the sight
of seven brown pelicans, flying in a loopy line
across our wake.

Evening Rain

Rain sounds on the roofs of trees
and the complacent gravel,
is welcomed by everything green and ripened
coming from the ground.

It sounds the call of autumn
and just as swiftly as it comes, departs,
leaving a chorus of crickets
and this mute sighing for all that's gone —

summer moons,
scent of lemons,
the body of desire meeting itself.

Something hidden ruffles in the branches
and then, this breathing in again
for all that's fresh,

unspoken.

Bonsai

One cascades
from a mountain —
waterfall juniper.

Another frames fall
in an oval tray —
leaves staccatoed with yellow
and red, and all of them

waving in the breeze
like mismatched, shrunken
mittens.

But this one — winter pear —
miniature green fruit
cheeked with crimson,

so perfect,
so pellucid in its utility,

glows

Praising Names

Because they're vital for whispering in each other's ears,
for proffering salutations and greetings,
for identifying accuser and accused,
forgiver and forgiven.

Because they confer music: *Theresa*,
meaning "late summer," when the juice of blackberries
dribbles from the lips of children,
and sunlight drapes itself across a wooden table.
Havel or *Abel*, meaning "breath,"
the unrolling of the world like spooled ribbon.

Because they offer a sense of comfort,
like a room we know well,
can tell where the wallpaper has come undone,
where we've stashed a gold cross, or cash,
where we would dwell, if not
for the roofless nature that prompts us to look up —
at the darkening light, stars, or Arctic clouds drifting by.

Because when we leave behind summer and breath
and all the rest, the music of our names will linger
like an unfettered riff — a Coltrane solo —
floating,
blue,
and cool as stone.

Bright Morning

1.
Where is the altar if not before me now —
scattered books, yellow button chrysanthemums
in a jar on the desk,
the span between one footstep and the next?

2.
Not much frost on the roofs this morning, but cold.
Those hopping birds in the junipers
don't know anything about right or wrong.
Sunlight slants across the floor.
Sifting through passages on impermanence,
already much has slipped away —
parents,
friends and lovers,
the last of the plums.

3.
Who is this poem for if not the everyone in me,
the me in everyone?
Looking for that one somewhere else is foolish.
The hidden fool is nearer than my pills, pillow —
wisdom a rumor.

Ladder

This other ladder is made of bone,
is not a ladder at all, exactly,
but something climbs there and falls.

It rises and falls, lingering beside cinders
and sparks.
It doesn't sing, necessarily, but when it does,

singer and song lift like steam together,
drifting among the incidental clouds
in all their luminosity,

which is theirs only out of convenience,
which is, more exactly, unowned,
drifting.

Why We Sing in the Shower

First comes the ritual unwrapping,
the peeling away,
and then the familiar scent

that makes us sink
as if in a pool of ambergris and mint,
and maybe parapropylene.

Mornings, we take this
demon lover in our hands,
letting it caress us

as we reach for the shapes of our bodies,
feeling for what's been bruised,
what's been lost,

letting its blind latherings cleanse us,
if not of our scars, then at least
of yesterday's sweat —

renewing us — even as the familiar
feel of the other wears thin
and deliquesces

as most any lover would.

In the Antique Store Yesterday,

we ogled at a still-life of apricots, possibly by Cezanne
or, more likely, by someone painting in the style of the master,
a student or someone catering to tourists.
An expert was coming the following day, the owner said,
and that would settle the matter once and for all.

Afterwards, walking down the street with its well-kept yards
like the neat transliteration of Cezanne,
it rose up before us: a gnarled apricot tree
as high as our heads, dripping synchronicity
from every branch.

We knew it was real but reached out to reassure ourselves,
touching the downy orbs, not quite ripe yet.
And now this poem, reminding me of that,
how each of us springs like fruit from an ancient branch,
sparks of original fire,

how doubt opens into the appearance of the beautiful,
how appearance is mirrored in the light of the mind.

Butter and Egg Days

These are days of celebration in the town to the north of us,
for the milk that sustains us and the butter we make of it,
for the warmth of a spotted brown egg and the egg itself,

for shiny roosters and auburn hens in their yard,
for dark-eyed cows, grazing in the field,
for shearers of sheep and keepers of goats,

for builders of barns and coops and troughs,
for rabbits in the tomatoes and owls in the rafters,
for flowering apple trees, apricot, plum, and pear,

for avocados and almonds, walnuts and lychees,
for cranky blackbirds who feast in their rows,
for earthworms and butterflies, ants and gnats,

for bees and keepers of bees,
for all those who farm and harvest,
and those who partake of the harvest —

may all flourish, may all flourish.

In the Lobby of Hotel Paradise

The orchids in the lobby are fading
as fast as we are, but appear suspended
in their hexagonal basket, woven
by anonymous hands out of light and dark.
Their freshly made-up faces are slightly wan
with traces of lipstick and liner,
welcoming all who come in off the street
with a wink of paradise,
what may well have been here before all this,
steel, glass, and the inevitable marble —
that and the call of "Taxi!, Taxi!,"
echoing through the air-conditioned air,
like a parrot calling for its neon mate.

Up a Creek

Isn't this the happy element you've forgotten,
not youth itself but setting out along strange creeks
like this one, banked with anise and yellow broom?
Not discovering but discovered by a pool of tadpoles,
and then the two of you passing through the cool tunnel
under the highway into the cemetery —

you, wanting to go on, to visit markers of the dead
if not the dead themselves,
your little friend stricken with the forbidden-ness
of this unknown island you're bound to enter,
although later, much later,
and separately.

Beginnings

Before beginnings are endings and after those
the moment just before beginnings,
when all things are as if waiting for movement
in a leafless tree, which is really not a tree
but a history of defunct stars,
and everything is dark with the kind of dark
that can't be known except in dreams,
the kind of dark that small birds illumine
in the morning as I move to the window
to watch them in the greening air,
knowing again what day means
with song still in it, thank goodness.

Persimmon Tree

Last year the charcoal branches of the persimmon tree
dipped over the fence into the schoolyard,
dotted with quick brushstrokes of bitter orange
and teeming with blackbirds, feasting
on windfall fruit.

What year was it when the tree was so laden,
a silent explosion of color,
that I stood dumbstruck before it?
A hand-lettered sign —
                    PERSIMMONS $1 A DOZEN —
was taped to a cardboard box
and a woman in a white bandana
waited for customers.
                    Who remembers?

It's early yet, December-brisk.
I watch as two blackbirds arrive noisily
                    in the upper branches.
The lower ones have been cut back, almost to the trunk,
and the fruit — what there is of it,
maybe six or seven pieces — is high-up,
pale, and probably hard as stone.

Whoever comes here looking for sugar or fire
will be disappointed, I think, wanting the feast,
the bright pulp of amazement,
not settling easily in the leaves,
                    shimmering
like torn silk,
immune to ordinary light
and the brassy voices of the blackbirds
before they fly off into the filmy eye of winter.

Some Ways into Joy

1.
A few poems utter out like a bevy of moths
from the unbarricaded morning.
And isn't this surprising?
You're the boy in the yellow scarf
and the woman in the polka dot dress on Geary Street,
equally loved.

2.
Not so much the drawing of an amaryllis
as the dusty glint around it.
Not so much the wet sparrows
as the rain that ignites us.
It speaks of mythic kings and the soft part
of a child's skull,
the way we come and go.

3.
In ways known and unknown,
you've come to imagine yourself
as both mother and child,
love and the renewal of love.
Faith, that is, in milk and in blood,
the sanctity of touch.

Milkweed Wishes

Propped up against the chimney, split bamboo —
rolled and leaning there
for how many years now I don't know —
weathered the same gray as this overcast morning.

Fitting foils for the random detail: spiraling up
from cracked concrete, a milkweed,
graced with a handful of yellow flowers
no bigger than a nickel

and as many fingernail pods,
their delicate geometry partially flown
like inchoate prayers to the god
of minor miracles.

Are past, present, and future contained
in the wish-fulfilling orbs? And if they are,
what do I wish for, now that the other wishes
are lived-out, or unanswered?

Waves and waves of yellow flowers
and as many amber-colored lives swarming about,
so many that two or three will land on a boy's arm
or wrist — sometimes, but not always,

letting him stroke their peach-fuzz wings.

Blackbirds in December

I watch as wet blackbirds glitter and bounce
in the pyracanthus, avoiding thorns,
and clutching in their beaks
the blood red berries,
before swallowing them whole.

What luck for them to have it here, I think,
this tangled home, although
more than once I've been stuck
when trimming back untamed branches.
and bled.

But what good it brings,
watching blackbirds in the pyracanthus,
watching them dart and fly
in and out of the branches, and praying
they don't slam themselves against the window,

hard, as they sometimes do,
                            falling,
then quickly coming-to in the junipers,
then swerving, cockeyed, over the fence —
quite drunk, the little gluttons, at Christmastide.

Self

Why not call it moonlight
between apple branches,

then find something you call
a stone or a feather

and rename it again and again,
as namer and named dissolve

in darkness, reappear
as river silt, the pale green

husk of corn, paw prints
on snow, a fox's —

all of them evading the fables
of meaning,

all of them radiant
with the moon's elixir.

Dry Spell

1.
I hope it rains soon, a good long February rain.
That's the only thing I can think of that will cheer me up:
the sound of rain puddling in the garden,
hitting the windows — songs of purification.

2.
I know I can't give life to the dying,
or buy the moon,
but the smoky clouds give me hope
that all will be well after a rain.

3.
All about us, grasses, stones, roofs, fences, roads
are dry with age, ready to break like old hips.
When the rain comes it will fill our lips to overflowing.
We will speak in tongues of journeys to the sea.

Something of What Was

remains: this time it's the bolt
from the repaired gate
and a screw, rusted almost to oblivion.

Another time it was spectacles,
and once, letters, written in perfect script,
tied together with something like string,
kite string, or a strong twine.

The carpenter must have left them here,
unthinkingly, on the patio table —
the bolt and screw, I mean —
right next to the blackened lemon,

the one that fell weeks ago
and no one, not I,
or anyone,
knew what to do with.

White Poppies

Tell Shelley the *dwarf ivories* are here,
sending out their runners
and spreading canticles of light
across the parched fields of summer.

Hardly anyone notices, the flowers are so small,
about the size of quarters and tilted to the center,
so that they might hold a child's attention
or anything close to the ground

like the moth-like butterflies, speckled
orange and black, that cruise around them,
their translucent petals more like lenses, really,
through which the world imagines itself.

And if they could speak,
I think they might tell us something about happiness,
how unprepossessing it is —
a slip of a thing, easily missed.

About holding close to the earth
as you would a lover, tracing with your fingers
a history of mornings, much like this one,
across the body's forgotten places.

Acknowledgements

My thanks to the editors of those journals in which the following poems first appeared, sometimes in slightly different forms:

White Poppies: *Crosswinds Poetry Journal*, 2018
Pulling Weeds: *The Curlew*, June 2018; Wales, U.K.
Looking Out at the Stream: *Albatross*, 2018
Ekphrasis: World Enough Writers *Last Call: The Anthology of Beer, Wine & Spirits Poetry*, 2018
The Soul Longs for Home: *ARTS*, 2018
December Mushrooms: *Dodging the Rain* (IE), December, 2017 (online)
Pieces, Some Blue: *Poet Lore*, 2017
Bonsai: *Roaring Muse*, 2017
The Good Knot: *Spiritus*, Spring, Vol. 17.1, 2017
Some Ways into Joy: *Reed Magazine*, 2017
Crow Makes a Scene: *Awake in the World*, A Riverfeet Press Anthology, 2017
First Frost: *Contemporary Poetry – an Anthology of Present Day Best Poems*, Vol. 3, 2017
Spotting Turkeys, Persimmon Tree: *Crosswinds Poetry Journal*, 2016
Uncertain Fire: *Passager*, Summer, 2016
Self: *Xanadu*, Long Island Poetry Collective, 2016
Cranking the Wheel: *Crab Creek Review*, Fall, 2015
Joice Street Steps, Crossings: *Archaeopteryx*, 2014

Gratitude, also, to the editors of Finishing Line Press, for permission to reprint selections from the chapbook, *Spell of the Ordinary* (January, 2018).

About the Author

Jerome Gagnon is the author of *Rumors of Wisdom* from Concrete Wolf Press, and a chapbook, *Spell of the Ordinary*, from Finishing Line Press. A graduate of San Francisco State University's Creative Writing Program, his poetry has appeared in a variety of journals, including *Poet Lore, Spiritus, Crab Creek Review, Archaeopteryx,* and several anthologies. In addition to winning the Louis Poetry Book Award, his poem "Cherries, After" received the 2018 Robert Frost Poetry Prize, sponsored by the Frost Foundation.

His work reflects a life-long interest in eastern poetry and the contemplative arts. Scholar and poet Mark S. Burrows has observed that the poems in *Rumors of Wisdom* are "rooted in the patience of deep and thoughtful looking and pondering." Editor and poet Lana Hechtman Ayers has written of *Spell of the Ordinary* that, "Here you will find beauty in discord and discard, loveliness in the moment and in the minute."

In 2012 he received an M.A. in English/TESOL from California State University East Bay, while teaching and tutoring a diverse group of speakers. Now retired, he lives in Northern California.

www.ingramcontent.com/pod-product-compliance
Lightning Source LLC
Chambersburg PA
CBHW030457010526
44118CB00011B/972